All The Minor Things

a collection of poems

Arlo Lokomaika'i

/ BookLeaf
Publishing
India | USA | UK

Made with ❤ on the BookLeaf Publishing Platform
www.bookleafpub.in
www.bookleafpub.com

Dedication

To Hannah, Alex, Tai, Edgar, Kukui, Jade, Jasmine, Mom, Dad. Thank you for putting up with my chaos, albeit somewhat. To others that have heard me out at work, my other pals, thank you for keeping me sane.

Preface

After a certain amount of time, there will be way too much reflection for the average person. If a whole mess of crazy happens within a year, well, let's hope you can write about it too. Welcome to the thunder dome.

Acknowledgements

To the ones that picked up this book not totally knowing what to expect, I hope you find some peace and growth added to your being. To the ones that have stayed and endured my heart, know you mean the most to me.

frontal lobe

I wanted the world
I wanted the breathe of life, the **Ha**
I wanted to feel like I mattered.

We tended to our gardens in different ways,
different sowing patterns, different seeds, different
amounts of sunlight
different symphonies played to help us grow

I just didn't know how intricate our leaves intertwining
would make everything be.

I was too scared to grow my garden without security
but I was only limiting what I could do for you.

Losing you took the sunlight away,
the music dulled,
the colors dried,
my heart
my love

faded

what I make and what I play will only take me away for
a moment,
when you took me away for longer.

I know I am not the one who walked away, not the one
who chose this,
but I always know it would be for the best, for you.

50 mph isnt as fast as you think it is

I ran far far away
so far that the horizon couldn't find me
I drove past the streets
where we shared little treats
and secret sheets

I couldn't feel the numbing cold that hit my face, night
after night
I found the stars to be a comfort
a home

They twinkled brighter than any type of light
any type of direction
Shone brighter than the moon
the one we always looked forward too.

I avoid parks now.
Gazebos that are overgrown with green, too good to be
true.

I avoid slow songs that make me think of you,
and what could've been.

I don't avoid reflection
or the repercussions of my choices

My greatest revenge will be me becoming who I
promised you I would be, even if you won't ever see it.

growth

I've had the opportunity to watch the sky change
Bright blues, dreamy purples, wondrous oranges

I watched as the leaves sprouted, bloomed
Turn yellow, fall
Turn brown, and crunch.

I watched as the wind moved the fluffy clouds
The arms of the trees that shielded me from the storms

I listened for the voices that came,
The cadence that changed
The draft I felt whispering goosebumps into my brain

I saw the flowers in their brightest hues
And most fragrant dews
Wilt and turn,
Only to die.

The cycle is big,

Obvious.
So is mine.

With the pills,
With the talks,
With the coping skills,
With knowing what's at stake if I lose.

Knowing my own worth and my boundaries
That,
That makes my heart feel full again.

feeling small

Spikes prickling on my skin
Breathing so thin

Where is the fire that's lit within?

Eyes dart across the room,
Searching,
Needing,
knowing escape.

Hands clutch tighter and tighter
Needing to feel looser and looser
Need to hear that its okay

Not everything is going to be aflame

Convincing the body,
Calming it down,
Centering the space again

Breathe.

Breathe.

Focus,

Breathe.

This too shall pass.

kukui.

He had the brightest eyes
And the softest fur
Always felt the need to speak when he saw you.

5 years.
I see him when I hear a door creak,
Imagining a little pitter patter on the floor.
5 years.
I hear him when we play songs
The music videos he used to sing along too.

Yes, we only had him for 5 years
Those are the years I tried to live
Years I tried to move on from the fires and tumultuous
waves
years I WANTED to be alive.

I cradled you on the bad days,
when you would lick up my tears.
Laughed and played with you on the good days,

and felt everything between.

You showed me that I had empathy,
and you still show me that I never have to give that up.

E ho'omaha me ka Maluhia, sweet boy.

persona

Crisp clean October air
Or as "clean" as we're going to tell ourselves it'll be...

That feeling when you slip into a sweater when the wind
bites at your being.

The touch of something fuzzy, keeping you warm.

Fresh laundry, on a day you're off from work.
Static clings
Like an uninhibited choice
like a liberated tongue

I envelop myself into my own personal hug,
cold,
empty.

Just give it time.

No longer home where the heart is,

No longer home at all.

What's in a home anyway?

and when will I finally find where I feel that feeling?

When can I come home?

apathy.

You know, I never will find it within myself to hate you.

Melancholy,
Homeless,
As poor as a church mouse,
Pulling from an already dried up well.

It's fair that you chose to walk (make me this way) away.

We never made it to 'Til Death Do Us Part,
And thank GOD
because I was too broken for you

I let the darker days get the best of me
Grab a hold and choke out my flame
until all I could see were the Stars

I forgot what it meant to be a lover,
And no, I am no saint,
I am not innocent at all,

but I got the help.
I got the fix.

It was already too late.

Already far gone.

I'm sorry for all the strife I caused,
And you can hate me all you want,
avoid and cut me out like the viper I am.
Hell will freeze over before you could ever want to
forgive me.

But that's okay.
Neither of us are innocent,
and like you've always said,
You always get what you want.

I hope you want peace, happiness, and good health.
cuz that's all I wish for you.

tally up the places I've slept

plush

leather

creaky cots

springs that loaded straight into my spine

full of holes

wet

dry

dark

light

Safe, warm, finally,
new era begins.

to all the homies I've loved before.

A friend once told me...

it doesn't matter how long you know someone, that does not make them your friend. It's the shit they do for you that counts.

I'm sure that's a quote somewhere from someone that matters much more than me
But the hole that my heart has felt since then

The longing
The loneliness

I can pick back up and move on.
It's not the first time this has happened,
But I will make sure it is my last.

I will adjust my expectations
I will curb my appetite for community

I will know who to give my loyalty too and when to act.

I already put me first.

Took too damn long to get there.

descent.

I will not be your laughing stock
Not something for you to poke

I will not be your saving line
The punchline to your joke

I know what I love,
who I care for.

I know what I need
I am no bore.

I live forever unapologetically
Happily, kinectically

I have lived for far too long
to swallow your words

I have a choice

and I've made it,
with or without any of you

mums the word

I am terrified of you.

Never breaking eye contact,
Always confident in what you are saying or doing,
Daring anyone to make you think different.

You've been there to lift makeup in low times,
And of course can't help but love the way the stars make
your voice warmer
And your eyes shinier

But its that.
Eyes.
God, they terrify me.

For all the patterns shown
the music shown
the sky ever brighter

I will never be giving that a go.

the first step

Bright disco lights
Loud pulsing music
Coursing through my veins

I taste of too many "something fruitys"
And have concert aftermath all over me

I feel the liquor sitting in the system,
Watching the people dance in slow motion around me
I dance too,
Freeing,
Feeling a release I needed.

How did I get here?

Fellowship,
"Community"
Love?

No, Love is a big word.

Too big of a feeling.

Just a new chapter.

prosperity

crinkled up green
splitting at the seams
ones I created
the type you can't make clean

two dollar bills are supposed to be lucky.
Something about the rarity of it.
Good fortune, good things come in pairs
The number two

Mine has been kept in my pocket,
Day in and day out

And trust me,
I'm still waiting for the luck to kick in.

But I can breathe again.

process

Burnt coffee
Stinging my tongue
I haven't seen these gray walls in a long time

My mind is always running
One prompt to the other
Over and over again

The stinging words of the past
The things I should've said and done instead
Eating away causing the pounding to never end
The biting past of toxicity that will never happen again

Moving figures in the corner of my eyes
I'm never truly alone.
Apathetic tendencies
Kicking into my forever home.

I want to be the type of person who shows up and sticks
around

I want to be the type of person who isn't too hard to love
Too hard to have relations

But these orange bottles knock me out
Like a tranquilizer
Is this the only way to get them to stop?
Sleeping away the pain
Just to feel sane?

planned parenthood

I wanted to live somebody else's dream
someone who could conceive and have a family with
unfaltering love
what was my dream?
who was in it?

It was what I was **supposed** to want
what I was **expected** to be like
but from who?

I tricked myself for so long before I found what I really
wanted.

No more expectations.
Embrace my own life.
only willing and being acceptant
to my own plan

i prefer watermelon on hot summer days.

I am not someone of certain descent
that leaves a rough taste to the ones that are meant
to stand up and change
and rage

I am, however, descent
of native Hawaiians that support
cousins, brothers, sisters of all
we stick together when we are at a fall

Destroying families and lives
No way to have perfect ties
You rip and tear and watch as people suffer
While pretending Tylenol can be a buffer.

Disgusting lies
Perceiving eyes
There's nothing that can be right.

Breathe with me
Scream with me

There's so much more out there than just us.

Now make that change.

You are on Native Land.

Ku Kia'i Mauna.

we were meant to be a lesson.

sunkissed skin
hot but cold air
little whispers of another life

I close my eyes and I can feel
see
embrace
different versions of me

I can finally say I am comfortable in my own skin
Maybe what happened needed too
Sure, yes, I'll go with that.

Some cycles renew,
Most will not.

I have left so much in this year,
and it has only made me stronger
and fuller

and I can *see* now.

there is no "replacing" or "renewing"

only space for what is deemed worthy,
and those expectations have changed.

karma chameleon

my bark is loud
but my bite is deep

I could never be what I didn't want to be.

whether that was with you, dear,
or with the ones who knew me much longer,
perhaps even the ones who knew me my whole life.

No, that was never going to be me.

I can't wait for you to see them though.

numb

I could never really handle death that well
for the people I truly loved and cared for
when their time was up it killed a part of me.

I would be told last sometimes
when it came to things like that
you cry too much and it becomes what you're known for

I have no tears left to spill for anything anymore
my heart can ache,
but it can no longer fill that hole of empathy that has
been emptied for far too long.

I miss so many people that have come and gone
and there's nothing wrong with that

Just a closed chapter that I can look back on,
not causing anything to have too much of a reaction.

I'm getting too grown for that.

louder for the ones in the back

I would rather make myself slightly uncomfortable just for you to feel a little less lonely.

Have hope for a day.

Pehea 'oe?

I hope you have a great day.

May you succeed in all your endeavors.

bite

throw me under the bus
run me over
watch as my limbs smack against the ground,
let the concrete eat me up

chew me up
spit me out
make me unrecognizable

I will get up again,
fix myself,
and continue on.

I will not let anyone win
not over me

Determination is key.
Confidence is the booster.
And, well,
isn't that just sexy?

.